just
cocktails

140 Recipes for Fun and Festive Cocktails

JG PRESS

Library of Congress Cataloging-in-Publication Data is available upon request.

ISBN: 978-1-57215-702-6 (cloth); 978-1-57215-736-1 (cloth)

Printed in China.

10 9 8 7 6 5 4 3 2 1

contents

Basic Recipes

Simple Syrup (makes ⅓ cup)

Sugar syrup is needed in a good cocktail bar, as sugar will not dissolve easily in cold cocktails.

    2 oz water
    1 cup sugar

Place sugar and water in a saucepan and bring to a boil. Reduce heat and simmer gently for approximately 5 minutes until the mixture condenses into a clear, sweet syrup. Cool.

Note: You can use immediately or store indefinitely in a sealed container in the refrigerator.

Sweet-and-Sour Mix (makes 5 cups)

Sweet-and-sour mix, also known as bar mix, is an important part of many cocktails.

1 egg white (optional)
1 cup sugar
2 cups water
2 cups fresh lemon juice

1   Whisk one egg white until frothy in a medium bowl.

2   Mix in the sugar, then the water and lemon juice. Beat until all the sugar is dissolved.

Note: The egg whites are optional, but will make the drinks slightly foamy. Will keep in refrigerator for about a week.

Mixing Methods

SHAKE

To mix by shaking in a cocktail shaker by hand. Fill the glass part of the shaker three-quarters full with ice, then pour the ingredients on top. Pour the contents of the glass into the metal part of the shaker and shake vigorously for 10–15 seconds. Remove the glass section and, using a Hawthorn strainer, strain contents into the cocktail glass. Shaking ingredients that do not mix easily with spirits is easy and practical, for example, juices, egg whites, cream and sugar syrups.

STIR

To mix the ingredients by stirring them with ice in a mixing glass and then straining them into a chilled cocktail glass. Short circular twirls are most preferred (the glass part of a shaker will do well for this). Spirits, liqueurs and vermouths that blend easily together are mixed by this method.

BUILD

To mix the ingredients in the glass in which the cocktail is to be served, floating one on top of the other. Highball, long fruit juice and carbonated mixed cocktails are typically built using this technique. Where possible, a swizzle stick should be put into the drink to mix the ingredients after being presented. Long straws are excellent substitutes when swizzle sticks are unavailable.

BLEND

To mix the ingredients using an electric blender or mixer. Add the fruit first (using small pieces of fruit gives a smoother texture), then pour in the alcohol. Ice should always be added last. This order ensures that the fruit is blended freely with the alcoholic ingredients and allows the ice to gradually mix in, chilling the drink. Ideally, the blender should be on for at least 20 seconds.

Always check that the blender is clean before you start. Angostura bitters is ammonia-based, so it's suitable for cleaning. Fill with hot water, rinse and then wipe clean.

Stocking Your Cocktail Bar

Again, be guided by buying the ingredients that you need for your favorite cocktails if you do not have the space or the resources to purchase the whole list.

Recommended spirits

Brandy

Campari

Gin

Malibu

Ouzo

Pernod

Rum, dark and light

Southern Comfort

Tequila

Vodka

Whiskey, for example, Scotch whisky, Irish whiskey, rye whiskey, Tennessee whiskey, Bourbon

Recommended Vermouth

Vermouth bianco

Vermouth dry

Vermouth rosso

Recommended liqueurs

Advocaat

Amaretto

Baileys Irish Cream

Banana Liqueur

Benedictine

Curaçao blue

Chartreuse, green and yellow

Cherry advocaat

Cherry brandy

Coconut liqueur

Cointreau

Crème de cacao

Crème de café

Crème de cassis

Crème de menthe

Drambuie

Frangelico

Galliano

Grand Marnier

Grenadine cordial (non-alcoholic)

Kahlúa

Kirsch

Mango liqueur

Melon liqueur

Orange liqueur
Peach liqueur
Pimm's No. 1
Sambuca black
Sambuca clear
Strawberry liqueur
Tia Maria
Triple sec
Vandermint

Juices, garnishes and other ingredients

Almonds, slivered
Apple
Apricot jelly
Banana
Blueberries
Cantaloupe
Carbonated water
Celery
Celery salt
Chocolate flakes
Cinnamon
Cocktail onions, red
Coconut cream
Cream, fresh, single and whipped
Cucumber
Eggs
Fruit, canned
Fruit nectar, canned
Fruit pulp, canned
Jelly babies
Lemon juice, pure
Lemons
Limes

Maraschino cherries, red
Milk
Mint leaves
Nutmeg
Olives
Onions
Orange and mango juice
Oranges
Pepper
Pineapple, canned crushed
Pineapple, fresh
Salt
Strawberries
Sugar and sugar cubes
Sugar syrup
Tabasco
Tomatoes
Vanilla ice cream
Worcestershire sauce

1

classic cocktails

Champagne Cocktail ▸

Serves 1

    1 sugar cube
    6 drops Angostura bitters
    ½ oz cognac
    4 oz Champagne
    maraschino cherry

Soak sugar cube in Angostura bitters in the flute before adding cognac. Top with Champagne and garnish with a cherry.

Kir Royal

Serves 1

    ½ oz crème de cassis
    Champagne

Pour crème de cassis into glass, then top up with chilled Champagne, no ice.

Note: Kir Imperial is made with grenadine and crème de cassis plus Champagne.

French 75 ▸

Serves 1

> 1 oz gin
> 2 oz Sweet-and-Sour Mix (see p. 4)
> Champagne

B uild over ice in glass and stir lightly. Top with Champagne.

Twelfth Night Champagne

Serves 1

> slice of lime
> superfine sugar
> 1 oz Grand Marnier
> ¹/₂ slice of lemon
> ¹/₂ slice of orange
> dry Champagne

R ub lime slice around rim of Champagne flute, then frost rim of glass with sugar. Pour Grand Marnier into glass, drop the two slices of fruit in and top up with chilled Champagne.

Sangria ▸

Serves 10

1 bottle dry red wine (chilled)
2 oz brandy
2 oz white rum
2 oz Cointreau or triple sec
4 cups orange juice
2 teaspoons sugar
selection of chopped fruit, such as apples, pears, melon, or berries

Combine all ingredients in a large punch bowl. Chill. Add 4 cups ice cubes, serve in cocktail glasses.

Buck's Fizz

Serves 1

5 oz Champagne
$\frac{1}{2}$ oz Cointreau
1 oz orange juice
$\frac{1}{2}$ teaspoon grenadine
slice of orange

Pour all ingredients except grenadine and orange slice into chilled Champagne flute. Drop the grenadine into center of the drink and stir well. Garnish with the orange slice and serve with a straw.

Bullfrog ▸

Serves 1

1¹/₂ oz vodka
¹/₂ oz triple sec
6 oz lemonade or limeade
slice of lemon or lime

Pour the vodka, triple sec and lemonade or limeade into a highball glass filled with ice and stir well. Garnish with a slice of lemon or lime.

Moscow Mule

Serves 1

1¹/₂ oz vodka
1 oz lime juice
¹/₂ cup ginger soda
lime wedge

Combine all liquid ingredients in a highball glass filled with clean ice cubes and stir well. Garnish with the lime wedge.

Bay Breeze ▶

1½ oz vodka
3 oz pineapple juice
1 oz cranberry juice
wedge of pineapple

Combine liquid ingredients over ice in a highball glass and stir well. Garnish with a wedge of pineapple.

Karoff

Serves 1

1½ oz vodka
1 oz cranberry juice
5 oz club soda
lime wedge

Combine all liquid ingredients in a highball glass filled with ice and stir well. Garnish with the lime wedge.

Salty Dog ▸

Serves 1

2 teaspoons salt
wedge of lime
2 oz vodka
5 oz grapefruit juice

Place the salt in a saucer. Rub the lime wedge around the rim of a highball glass. Dip the glass into the salt to coat the rim. Almost fill the glass with ice cubes and pour the vodka and grapefruit juice into the glass. Stir well.

Greyhound

Serves 1

1 oz vodka
grapefriut juice
lemon twist to garnish

Combine ingredients in a highball glass filled with ice, stir and serve, garnished with lemon twist.

Harvey Wallbanger ▸

Serves 1

1¹/₂ oz vodka
4 oz orange juice
¹/₂ oz Galliano
slice of orange

Combine vodka and orange juice in a highball glass filled with ice and stir well. Float the Galliano on top. Garnish with a slice of orange.

Screwdriver

Serves 1

1¹/₂ oz vodka
1¹/₂ oz orange juice
slice of orange

Build over ice. Garnish with the orange.

Vodka Collins ▸

Serves 1

2 oz vodka
1 oz lemon juice
1 teaspoon sugar (superfine, if available)
3 oz club soda
maraschino cherry
slice of orange

Combine first three ingredients in a cocktail shaker with cracked ice. Shake well and strain into a highball glass almost filled with ice cubes. Add the club soda and stir. Garnish with a cherry and a slice of orange.

Tom Collins

Serves 1

2 oz gin
2 oz lemon juice
1 teaspoon sugar
3 oz club soda
maraschino cherry
slice of lemon

Combine first three ingredients in a cocktail shaker with cracked ice. Shake well and strain into a highball glass almost filled with ice cubes. Add the club soda and stir. Garnish with a cherry and a slice of lemon.

Bloody Mary ▸

Serves 1

1½ oz vodka
1½ teaspoons lemon juice
2 drops Worcestershire
2 drops Tabasco
salt and pepper to taste
tomato juice
celery stick, green olive or marinated string bean

Combine liquid ingredients over ice in a highball glass and stir well. Garnish with vegetable of choice.

Bloody Maria

Serves 1

⅛ teaspoon black pepper
2½ oz tequila
⅛ teaspoon celery salt
5 oz tomato juice
1 dash Tabasco sauce
½ oz lemon juice
1 stick of celery, to garnish

In a shaker half-filled with ice, combine all of the ingredients except the garnish. Shake well, then strain into a highball glass almost filled with ice cubes. Garnish with a stick of celery and a straw.

Beer Buster ▸

Serves 1

1½ oz vodka
2 dashes Tabasco
12 oz beer

Stir vodka and Tabasco together in a chilled beer mug or pint glass. Pour in beer.

Red Eye

Serves 1

5 oz cold beer
5 oz tomato juice
½ cherry tomato

Pour tomato juice into glass, add beer and serve.

Kamikaze ▶

Serves 1

1½ oz vodka
½ oz Cointreau or triple sec
2 teaspoons Rose's lime juice

Combine ingredients in a mixing glass filled with ice cubes. Stir well and strain into a cocktail glass.

Dusty Dog

Serves 1

2 oz vodka
½ oz crème de cassis
1 teaspoon lemon juice
dash bitters
5 oz ginger soda
lemon twist

Combine liquid ingredients in a cocktail shaker with cracked ice. Shake well and strain into a chilled highball glass almost filled with clean ice cubes. Garnish with the lemon twist.

Long Island Iced Tea ▸

Serves 1

>1 oz vodka
>1 oz gin
>1 oz light rum
>1 oz tequila
>1 oz lemon juice
>1 teaspoon sugar
>4 oz cola
>slice of lemon

Combine liquid ingredients except the cola in a cocktail shaker with cracked ice. Shake well and strain into a highball glass almost filled with ice cubes. Add the cola and stir well. Garnish with a slice of lemon.

Pimm's No. 1 Cocktail

Serves 1

>1 to 1½ oz Pimm's No. 1 Cup
>7-up or dry ginger ale
>orange slice
>cherry
>cucumber (skin on)

Build Pimm's over ice. Top-up with either 7-up or dry ginger ale or equal parts of both. Garnish with an orange slice, cherry, cucumber skin, swizzle stick and straws.

Notes: A slice of orange can detract from the sweet aftertaste. Slicing the inside of the cucumber skin allows the small drops to keep the drink chilled. Originally six types of Pimm's were commonly consumed, today there are only two: Pimm's No.1, which has a gin base, and Pimm's No. 2, which has a vodka base. Often referred to as the "Fruit Cocktail Cocktail."

Whiskey Sour ▸

Serves 1

1¹/₂ oz scotch whiskey
1 oz lemon juice
¹/₂ oz sugar syrup
¹/₂ egg white
slice of lemon
maraschino cherry

Shake all ingredients except lemon slice and cherry over ice, then strain into glass. Garnish with a slice of lemon and a cherry.

Lynchburg Lemonade

Serves 1

²/₃ oz Jack Daniel's Tennessee whiskey
²/₃ oz Cointreau
²/₃ oz fresh lime juice
7-up or soda water
1 strip lemon peel

Pour in order then top up with 7-up or soda water. Serve garnished with twisted lemon rind.

Note: This delicious cocktail originates from the home of Jack Daniel's.

Old-Fashioned ▸

Serves 1

2–3 dashes Angostura bitters
1 sugar cube
2 oz bourbon
club soda
slice of orange
slice of lemon

Splash bitters evenly over sugar cube before adding ice and bourbon. Top with club soda. Garnish with a slice of orange and lemon.

Rusty Nail

Serves 1

1 oz Scotch whisky
1 oz Drambuie
lemon twist

Build over ice. Garnish with the lemon.

Manhattan ▸

Serves 1

1½ oz rye whiskey
1½ oz sweet vermouth
dash of Angostura bitters
maraschino cherry

Combine liquid ingredients in a mixing glass with ice and stir well. Strain into a chilled martini glass and garnish with a cherry.

Americano

Serves 1

1 oz Campari
1 oz sweet vermouth
club soda
slice of orange

Build over ice and top up with club soda. Garnish with the orange slice on side of glass.

Mint Julep ▶

Serves 1

1 teaspoon sugar
3 dashes of club soda
5 sprigs fresh mint
2 oz bourbon

Muddle sugar, soda water and 4 mint sprigs in a glass. Pour into chilled glass packed with ice. Add bourbon and mix with a chopping motion using a long-handled bar spoon. Garnish with remaining mint and serve with a straw.

Pink Squirrel

Serves 1

$^1/_2$ oz crème de almond
$^1/_2$ oz white crème de cacao
2 oz heavy cream

Blend all ingredients with ice and strain into cocktail glass.

Black Russian ▸

Serves 1

> 2 oz vodka
> 1 oz Kahlua

Combine ingredients in an old-fashioned glass filled with crushed ice. Stir.

Godson

Serves 1

> 1 oz Galliano
> 1 oz amaretto
> 1 oz heavy cream
> cinnamon dust

Build over ice cubes in glass and stir. Sprinkle with cinnamon dust.

White Russian ▸

Serves 1

1¹/₂ oz vodka
1 oz Kahlua
1 oz light cream

Combine ingredients in a cocktail shaker with cracked ice. Shake well and strain into an old-fashioned glass almost filled with ice cubes.

Hot Buttered Rum

Serves 1

1 teaspoon brown sugar
1 tablespoon butter
2 oz dark rum
ground nutmeg

Place sugar in mug, pour over ½ cup hot water and stir well, then add butter and rum. Sprinkle nutmeg on top.

Brandy Alexander ▸

Serves 1

1 oz brandy
1 oz dark crème de cacoa
1 oz heavy cream
ground nutmeg
maraschino cherry

Combine brandy, crème de cacoa, and cream in a cocktail shaker over ice. Shake until chilled. Strain into glass and garnish with a dash of nutmeg and a cherry.

Hot Brandy Alexander

Serves 1

1 oz brandy
1 oz dark crème de cacao
4 oz hot (but not boiling) milk
whipped cream
chocolate flakes

Pour all ingredients except cream and chocolate into heated mug. Top with whipped cream and sprinkle with chocolate flakes.

Irish Coffee ▶

Serves 1

    wedge of orange
    sugar
    1½ oz Irish whiskey
    hot coffee
    whipped cream

Rub rim of glass with orange and frost with sugar. Pour Irish whiskey into glass and fill to within half inch of top with the hot coffee. Cover surface to brim with whipped cream.

Coffee Royal

Serves 1

    4 oz hot coffee
    1 teaspoon granulated sugar
    2 oz brandy
    2 oz heavy cream

Pour coffee in glass and add sugar, stir to dissolve. Add the brandy and stir well. Pour the cream carefully on top so that it floats.

Baileys Irish Coffee ▸

Serves 1

>   1 oz Baileys Irish Cream
>   1 teaspoon brown sugar
>   hot coffee
>   whipped cream
>   chocolate shavings

Pour Baileys into glass and stir in brown sugar. Top with hot coffee, leaving an inch for garnish of whipped cream and chocolate shavings.

Sombrero

Serves 1

>   1½ oz coffee liqueur
>   1 oz heavy cream

Shake all ingredients with ice and strain into a chilled snifter.

James Bond Martini

Gibson

Dirty Martini

Hot Stuff Martini

Gimlet

Vodka Gimlet

London Martini

Imperial

Perfect Martini

Red Gin

Opal Martini

Black and Silver

Parisian Martini

Portini

Dry Negroni

Sidecar

Licorice Martini

Copacabana

Fresh Lemon Martini

Citron Dragon

Cloister Martini

Palm Beach Martini

Cosmopolitan

Metropolitan

Flirtini

Caribbean Martini

Cherry Ripe

Seventh Heaven Martini

Deliberation

Dessert Shield

Apple Martini

Ante

Vanilla Wonder

Czarina

Fudgesicle

Almond Martini

Chocolate Martini

Butterscotch Martini

Chocolate Raspberry Martini

Death by Chocolate

Peppermint Martini

Golden Cadillac

martinis

2

James Bond Martini ▸

Serves 1

1½ oz gin
1½ teaspoon vodka
1½ teaspoon dry vermouth
lemon twist

Combine liquid ingredients with cracked ice in a cocktail shaker and shake well. Strain into a chilled martini glass and garnish with a lemon twist.

Gibson

Serves 1

2 oz gin
½ oz dry vermouth
1 white cocktail onion

Pour gin and vermouth into glass over ice and stir. Pierce onion with toothpick and drop into drink.

Dirty Martini ▸

Serves 1

1½ oz gin
½ oz dry vermouth
1½ teaspoons olive brine
2 stuffed cocktail olives

Combine liquid ingredients with cracked ice in a cocktail shaker and shake well. Rub rim of glass with lemon wedge. Strain liquid into a chilled martini glass and garnish with two olives.

Hot Stuff Martini

Serves 1

1½ oz gin or vodka
½ oz dry vermouth
dash of Tabasco
lime wedge

Combine liquid ingredients with cracked ice in a cocktail shaker and shake well. Strain into a chilled 3 oz martini glass and garnish with lime wedge. If a cocktail with more bite is desired, add another dash or two of Tabasco.

Gimlet ▸

Serves 1

2 oz gin
1/2 oz Rose's lime juice
wedge of lime

Combine all ingredients with cracked ice in a cocktail shaker and shake well. Strain into a chilled martini glass and garnish with a wedge of lime.

Vodka Gimlet

Serves 1

2 oz vodka
1/2 oz Rose's lime juice
wedge of lime

Combine all ingredients with cracked ice in a cocktail shaker and shake well. Strain into a chilled martini glass and garnish with a wedge of lime.

London Martini ▸

Serves 1

1½ oz gin or vodka
½ teaspoon maraschino liqueur
5 dashes orange bitters
½ teaspoon sugar (superfine, if available)
wedge of lemon

Combine liquid ingredients in a mixing glass and stir well. Pour mixture into a cocktail shaker with cracked ice and sugar, then shake well. Strain into a chilled martini glass and garnish with a wedge of lemon.

Imperial

Serves 1

1 oz gin
1 oz dry vermouth
dash of Angostura bitters
dash of maraschino liqueur
1 olive

Shake all liquid ingredients with ice and strain into cocktail glass. Spear the olive with a toothpick and add to the glass.

Perfect Martini ▶

Serves 1

1¹/₂ oz gin
1¹/₂ teaspoons dry vermouth
1¹/₂ teaspoons sweet vermouth
cocktail olive

Combine liquid ingredients with cracked ice in a cocktail shaker and shake well. Strain into a chilled 3 oz martini glass and garnish with an olive.

Red Gin

Serves 1

1¹/₂ oz gin
2 teaspoons cherry brandy
1 slice of orange

Shake all liquid ingredients with ice and strain into cocktail glass. Garnish with slice of orange speared with a toothpick.

Opal Martini ▸

Serves 1

1½ oz gin
1½ teaspoons Cointreau
½ oz fresh orange juice
¼ teaspoon sugar (superfine, if available)

Combine all ingredients with cracked ice in a cocktail shaker and shake well. Strain into a chilled martini glass.

Black and Silver

Serves 1

2 oz vodka
½ oz Chambord

Combine ingredients in a cocktail shaker with cracked ice and shake well. Pour into a chilled 3 oz martini glass.

Parisian Martini ▸

Serves 1

1¹/₂ oz gin
¹/₂ oz dry vermouth
1¹/₂ teaspoons crème de cassis
lemon twist

Combine all ingredients with cracked ice in a cocktail shaker and shake well. Strain into a chilled martini glass. Garnish with a lemon twist.

Portini

Serves 1

1¹/₂ oz gin
1¹/₂ teaspoons ruby port
2 teaspoons fresh lime juice
1 teaspoon grenadine
lime twist

Combine liquid ingredients with cracked ice in a cocktail shaker and shake well. Strain into a chilled 3 oz martini glass and garnish with lime twist.

Dry Negroni ▸

Serves 1

1 oz Campari
1 oz gin
1 oz dry vermouth
lemon twist

Combine all liquid ingredients in a glass almost filled with ice and stir well. Garnish with a lemon twist.

Sidecar

Serves 1

1 oz brandy
$^2/_3$ oz Cointreau
1 oz lemon juice
twist lemon rind

Shake all ingredients with ice and strain. Serve garnished with lemon rind.

Licorice Martini ▸

Serves 1

1½ oz gin or vodka
1½ teaspoon Pernod
1½ teaspoon anisette
½ teaspoon orange bitters
lemon twist

Combine liquid ingredients with cracked ice in a cocktail shaker and shake well. Pour over shaved ice into a martini glass and garnish with a lemon twist.

Copacabana

Serves 1

1 oz apricot brandy
½ oz lemon juice
½ oz brandy
½ oz Cointreau
crushed ice
orange wheel

Shake all ingredients and strain into a glass. Garnish with orange wheel.

Fresh Lemon Martini ▶

Serves 1

1½ oz vodka
1½ teaspoon triple sec
½ oz fresh lemon juice
1 dash orange bitters
cocktail olive

Combine liquid ingredients with cracked ice in a cocktail shaker and shake well. Strain into a chilled martini glass and garnish with an olive.

Citron Dragon

Serves 1

1½ oz Absolut citron vodka
½ oz Cointreau
1 oz melon liqueur
splash of soda
lemon twist to garnish

Combine liquid ingredients in a cocktail shaker with cracked ice and shake well. Pour into a chilled 5 oz cocktail glass. Garnish with a lemon twist.

Cloister Martini ▶

Serves 1

2½ oz gin or vodka
2 teaspoons grapefruit juice
1 teaspoon lemon juice
1 teaspoon yellow chartreuse
lemon zest

Combine all liquid ingredients with cracked ice in a cocktail shaker and shake well. Strain into a chilled martini glass. Add shaved ice if desired and garnish with fresh grated lemon zest.

Palm Beach Martini

Serves 1

1½ oz gin
1 teaspoon sweet vermouth
1 oz grapefruit juice

Combine all ingredients with cracked ice in a cocktail shaker and shake well. Strain into a chilled 3 oz martini glass.

Cosmopolitan ▶

Serves 1

1¹/₂ oz vodka
¹/₂ oz Cointreau
³/₄ oz cranberry juice
1¹/₂ teaspoons lime juice
lime twist

Combine liquid ingredients in a cocktail shaker with cracked ice and shake well. Pour into a chilled martini glass. Garnish with a lime twist.

Metropolitan

Serves 1

1¹/₂ oz gin
1¹/₂ teaspoons dry vermouth
¹/₂ oz fresh lime juice
lemon twist

Combine liquid ingredients with cracked ice in a cocktail shaker and shake well. Strain into a chilled 3 oz martini glass and garnish with lemon twist.

Flirtini ▸

Serves 1

1 oz vodka
2 oz Champagne
2 oz pineapple juice
wedge of pineapple

Combine all ingredients in a highball glass filled with ice, stir and garnish with a wedge of pineapple.

Caribbean Martini

Serves 1

granulated sugar
1½ oz light rum
1½ teaspoons dry vermouth
lime twist

Rim a chilled cocktail glass with sugar. Combine liquid ingredients with cracked ice in a cocktail shaker and shake well. Strain into a 3 oz martini glass and garnish with lime twist.

Cherry Ripe ▸

Serves 1

1½ oz vodka
½ oz cherry brandy
½ oz brandy
maraschino cherry

Combine liquid ingredients in a mixing glass filled with ice cubes. Stir well and strain into a martini glass and garnish with a cherry.

Seventh Heaven Martini

Serves 1

1½ oz gin or vodka
1½ teaspoons maraschino liqueur
1½ teaspoons grapefruit juice
fresh mint sprig

Combine liquid ingredients with cracked ice in a cocktail shaker and shake well. Strain into a chilled 3 oz martini glass and garnish with the mint sprig.

Deliberation ▸

Serves 1

1¹/₂ oz vodka
¹/₂ oz melon liqueur
lemon and lime twist

Combine ingredients in a mixing glass filled with ice cubes. Stir well and strain into a martini glass and garnish with a twist of lemon and lime.

Dessert Shield

Serves 1

1¹/₂ oz vodka
¹/₂ oz cranberry liqueur
¹/₂ cup cranberry juice

Combine ingredients in a highball glass filled with ice cubes. Stir well.

Apple Martini ▸

Serves 1

  2 oz vodka
  ½ oz apple schnapps
  ½ oz apple cider
  slice of apple

Combine liquid ingredients in a cocktail shaker with cracked ice. Shake well and strain into a chilled 5 oz cocktail glass. Garnish with a slice of apple.

Ante

Serves 1

  1 oz Dubonnet Rouge
  1 oz Calvados
  ½ oz Cointreau

Combine all ingredients in a mixing glass with ice and stir well. Strain into glass.

Vanilla Wonder ▸

Serves 1

3 oz vanilla-flavored vodka
1 oz white chocolate liqueur
maraschino cherry

Combine liquid ingredients in a cocktail shaker with cracked ice. Shake well and strain into a chilled martini glass. Garnish with a cherry.

Czarina

Serves 1

1 oz vodka
$\frac{1}{2}$ oz dry vermouth
$\frac{1}{2}$ oz apricot brandy
dash bitters

Combine ingredients in a mixing glass filled with ice cubes. Stir well and strain into a 3 oz martini glass.

Fudgesicle ▶

Serves 1

    1 oz vodka
    1¹/₂ teaspoons crème de cacao
    1¹/₂ oz chocolate syrup

Combine the ingredients in a shaker filled with ice, shake and serve in an old-fashioned glass filled with ice.

Almond Martini

Serves 1

    1¹/₂ oz vodka
    1¹/₂ teaspoons dry vermouth
    1¹/₂ teaspoons Frangelico
    roasted almonds

Combine liquid ingredients with cracked ice in a cocktail shaker and shake well. Strain into a chilled 3 oz martini glass and garnish with a few roasted almonds.

Chocolate Martini ▸

Serves 1

2 oz vodka
1 oz Godiva chocolate liqueur
cocoa powder
chocolate shavings

Wet rim of a martini glass and dip into cocoa powder. Combine vodka and chocolate liqueur in a cocktail shaker with ice. Shake well to chill. Strain into glass and garnish with chocolate shavings.

Butterscotch Martini

Serves 1

1$\frac{1}{2}$ oz vodka
$\frac{1}{2}$ oz butterscotch schnapps
$\frac{1}{2}$ oz butterscotch cream liqueur

Combine ingredients in a mixing glass with ice. Swirl gently and strain into a chilled cocktail glass.

Chocolate Raspberry Martini ▸

Serves 1

1½ oz vodka
½ oz Godiva chocolate liqueur
splash of club soda
raspberry

Combine vodka and chocolate liqueur ingredients in a cocktail shaker with cracked ice. Shake well and strain into a chilled martini glass. Top with a splash of club soda and garnish with a raspberry.

Death by Chocolate

Serves 1

1 oz Baileys Irish cream
1 oz crème de cacao
1 oz Kahlúa
3 oz whipping cream
1 oz Tia Maria
grated chocolate

Shake liquid ingredients with ice and strain into a champagne saucer. Garnish with grated chocolate and serve.

Peppermint Martini ▸

Serves 1

1¹⁄₂ oz vodka
¹⁄₂ oz white crème de menthe
fresh mint sprig

Combine liquid ingredients with cracked ice in a cocktail shaker and shake well. Strain into a chilled martini glass and garnish with a fresh mint sprig.

Golden Cadillac

Serves 1

1 oz Galliano Liqueur
1 oz white crème de cacao
1 oz fresh cream
red cherry or strawberry

Shake all ingredients with ice and strain into glass. Garnish with red cherry or strawberry.

Daiquiri	Tequila Sunrise
Frozen Daiquiri	Latin Lover
Mai Tai	Blue Hawaii
Banana Daiquiri	Frangelico Luau
Piña Colada	Electric Lemonade
Chiquita	Hawaiian Punch
Planter's Punch	Firefly
Devil's Tail	Tidal Wave
Singapore Sling	Fuzzy Navel
Bombay Punch	Freddy Fud Pucker
Bahama Mama	Chi Chi
Lights of Havana	Running Hot
Zombie	Banshee
Hurricane	Sail Away
Sex on the Beach	Almond Joy
Love Potion Number 9	Acapulco

3

tropical drinks

Daiquiri ▸

Serves 1

1½ oz white rum
1 oz fresh lemon juice
1½ oz Simple Syrup (see p. 4)
lemon twist

Combine rum, lemon juice and simple syrup in a cocktail shaker filled with ice. Shake until chilled, strain into champagne saucer or cocktail glass. Garnish with a lemon twist.

Frozen Daiquiri

Serves 1

1½ oz light rum
1 tablespoon Cointreau
1½ oz lime juice
1 teaspoon sugar
maraschino cherry

Blend all ingredients except the cherry with ½ cup crushed ice until smooth, then pour into cocktail glass. Garnish with cherry and serve.

Mai Tai ▸

Serves 1

1 oz white rum
$^1/_2$ oz amaretto
$^1/_2$ oz dark rum
1 oz orange curaçao
1 oz fresh lemon juice
1 oz Simple Syrup (see p. 4)
$^1/_2$ oz fresh lime juice
wedge of pineapple
maraschino cherry

Combine liquid ingredients in a cocktail shaker filled with ice. Shake until chilled and pour into cocktail glass. Garnish with a pineapple wedge and a cherry, serve with a straw.

Banana Daiquiri

Serves 1

1$^1/_2$ oz light rum
1 tablespoon Cointreau
1$^1/_2$ oz lime juice
1 teaspoon sugar
1 medium banana, sliced
lemon twist

Blend all ingredients except the lemon with ½ cup crushed ice until smooth, then pour into Champagne flute. Garnish with lemon twist.

Piña Colada ▸

Serves 1

1 oz light rum
1 oz crème de coconut
2 oz pineapple juice
pineapple spear

Blend rum, cream of coconut and pineapple juice with ice until mixed. Pour into glass and garnish with a pineapple spear. Serve with a straw.

Chiquita

Serves 1

1½ oz vodka
⅓ oz banana liqueur
⅓ oz lime juice
½ banana, sliced
pinch sugar
banana slice

Blend all ingredients with ice and pour into glass. Garnish with banana slice.

Planter's Punch ▸

Serves 1

> 1 oz dark rum
> 1/2 oz grenadine
> dash of Angostura bitters
> 1 1/2 Sweet-and-Sour Mix (see p. 4)
> club soda
> maraschino cherry

Shake first four ingredients over ice and strain into glass. Top with club soda and stir. Garnish with a cherry and serve with a straw.

Devil's Tail

Serves 1

> 1 1/2 oz light rum
> 1 oz vodka
> 1 1/2 teaspoons grenadine
> 1 1/2 teaspoons apricot brandy
> wedge of lime

Blend all liquid ingredients with 1/2 cup crushed ice until smooth. Pour into Champagne flute. Serve with a straw and garnish with lime wedge.

Singapore Sling ▸

Serves 1

1 oz gin
2 oz Sweet-and-Sour Mix (see p. 4)
½ oz grenadine
½ oz cherry brandy
maraschino cherry

Combine gin, sweet-and-sour mix and grenadine over ice. Top with cherry brandy and garnish with a cherry.

Bombay Punch

Serves 1

1 oz Cognac
½ oz dry sherry
½ oz Cointreau
½ oz maraschino liqueur
½ oz lemon juice
sparkling wine
red cherry

Blend first five ingredients with ice and pour into glass. Top up with sparkling wine and garnish with the red cherry. Serve with a straw.

Bahama Mama ▶

Serves 1

½ oz light rum
½ oz Malibu rum, or coconut-flavored rum
½ oz banana liqueur
½ oz grenadine
2 oz orange juice
2 oz pineapple juice
wedge of pineapple

Combine liquid ingredients with cracked ice and pour into glass. Garnish with a pineapple wedge and serve with a straw.

Lights of Havana

Serves 1

1½ oz Malibu
1 oz Midori melon liqueur
2 oz orange juice
2 oz pineapple juice
2 oz soda water
lime wheel

Shake all ingredients over ice and pour into glass. Garnish with a straw and a lime wheel.

Zombie ▸

Serves 1

- ½ oz white rum
- ½ oz Bacardi gold rum
- ½ oz dark rum
- ½ oz apricot brandy
- ½ oz overproof dark rum
- 2 oz pineapple juice
- ½ oz lime juice
- 1 teaspoon Simple Syrup (see p. 4)
- pineapple spear
- maraschino cherry
- mint leaves

Combine all liquid ingredients in cocktail shaker filled with ice. Shake until chilled and pour into cocktail glass. Garnish with a pineapple spear, a cherry and mint leaves.

Hurricane

Serves 1

- 1 oz Bacardi rum
- 1 oz passionfruit liqueur
- ½ oz lemon cordial
- 1½ oz lemon juice
- 1½ oz sugar syrup
- ½ oz Bacardi Gold rum
- crushed ice
- orange slice

Shake all ingredients except Bacardi with ice and pour into glass. Float in Bacardi Gold and garnish with orange slice.

Sex on the Beach ▸

Serves 1

1 oz vodka
1 oz peach schnapps
2 oz orange juice
2 oz cranberry juice
slice of orange

Combine all liquid ingredients in a highball glass filled with ice and stir well. Garnish with a slice of orange.

Love Potion Number 9

Serves 1

2$\frac{1}{2}$ oz Bacardi rum
$\frac{1}{2}$ egg white
1 oz Cointreau
$\frac{1}{2}$ oz lemon juice
maraschino cherry (optional)

Shake all ingredients with ice and strain into champagne saucer. Garnish with cherry and serve.

Tequila Sunrise ▶

Serves 1

2 oz gold tequila
4 oz fresh orange juice
³/₄ oz grenadine
maraschino cherry
slice of orange

Fill a highball glass halfway with ice. Add tequila, then orange juice. Insert a flat handled spoon into the glass. Add the grenadine quickly, allowing it to run down the back side of the spoon so it sinks to the bottom of the glass, creating a beautiful sunrise effect. Garnish with cherry and orange slice.

Latin Lover

Serves 1

1¹/₂ oz Champagne
2 teaspoons lemon juice freshly squeezed
3 dashes grenadine
1 oz tequila
crushed ice

Combine all ingredients in a shaker and shake well. Strain into an ice-filled old-fashioned glass.

Blue Hawaii ▸

Serves 1

1½ oz vodka
½ oz blue curacao
1½ teaspoons crème de coconut
4 oz pineapple juice

On the rocks: Combine ingredients in a shaker with ice. Shake until chilled and and strain into a small hurricane glass filled with crushed ice.

Blended: Combine ingredients with a scoop of ice in a blender. Mix well (15–20 seconds). Pour into a small hurricane glass.

Frangelico Luau

Serves 1

1½ oz Frangelico
7 oz pineapple juice
dash of grenadine
slice of pineapple

Blend first three ingredients with ice and pour into glass. Garnish with pineapple slice.

Electric Lemonade ▸

Serves 1

1½ oz vodka
½ oz blue curacao
2 oz Sweet-and-Sour Mix (see p. 4)
7Up or Sprite
maraschino cherry
slice of lemon

Combine all the liquid ingredients in a blender and blend for 15–20 seconds until smooth. Pour into a highball glass filled with ice. Garnish with a cherry and a slice of lemon.

Hawaiian Punch

Serves 1

⅔ oz Southern Comfort
⅔ oz Amaretto di Galliano
½ oz vodka
1½ oz pineapple juice
1½ oz orange juice
⅔ oz lime juice
⅔ oz grenadine
thin wedge of lime squeeze
thin wedge of lemon squeeze
slice of orange

Shake all ingredients except grenadine and fruits over ice and pour. Add grenadine. Garnish with squeeze of lime juice and lemon juice and slice of orange.

Firefly ▸

Serves 1

1¹/₂ oz vodka
2 oz grapefruit juice
dash of grenadine
maraschino cherry

Combine vodka and grapefruit juice in a highball glass filled with ice, add grenadine and stir. Garnish with a cherry.

Tidal Wave

Serves 1

1¹/₂ oz melon liqueur
1 oz orange juice
¹/₂ oz coconut liqueur
1¹/₂ oz Sweet-and-Sour Mix (see p. 4)
¹/₂ oz light rum
wedge of lime
maraschino cherry

Blend liquid ingredients with a cup of crushed ice until smooth. Pour into cocktail glass. Serve with a straw and garnish with lime slice and cherry on side of glass.

Fuzzy Navel ▸

Serves 1

1 oz vodka
1 oz peach schnapps
4 oz orange juice
slice of orange

Combine liquid ingredients in a highball glass filled with ice. Stir well. Garnish with a slice of orange.

Freddy Fud Pucker

Serves 1

1 oz tequila
4 oz orange juice
$1/_2$ oz Galliano
slice of orange
maraschino cherry

Build over ice in glass and float the Galliano on top. Garnish with the orange slice and cherry.

Chi Chi ▸

Serves 1

1½ oz vodka
2 oz pineapple juice
1 oz crème de coconut
½ banana
crushed ice
wedge of pineapple

Combine vodka, pineapple juice, crème de coconut and banana in a blender with crushed ice. Blend 20–30 seconds. Pour blended mixture into a highball glass. Garnish with a wedge of pineapple and umbrella.

Running Hot

Serves 1

1½ oz Bacardi rum
1½ oz pineapple juice
1 oz Cointreau
1 dash grenadine

Shake all ingredients and strain over ice into glass and serve.

Banshee ▸

Serves 1

½ oz banana liqueur
½ oz white crème de cacao
2 oz heavy cream

Combine all ingredients in a cocktail shaker filled with ice. Shake until chilled. Strain and serve in a cocktail glass.

Sail Away

Serves 1

1 oz Midori melon liqueur
1 oz lime juice
½ oz peach liqueur
1 dash lemon juice
1 oz vodka
ice cubes
lime wheel

Shake all ingredients with ice and strain into glass. Garnish with lime wheel to serve.

Almond Joy ▸

Serves 1

½ oz amaretto
½ oz white crème de cacao
2 oz heavy cream
maraschino cherry

Combine all ingredients in a cocktail shaker filled with ice. Shake until chilled, strain and garnish with a cherry.

Acapulco

Serves 1

1 oz tequila
1 oz dark rum
1 oz Tia Maria
5 oz coconut cream
orange slice

Shake ingredients in a shaker. Then strain over ice using a Hawthorn strainer into a 10 oz highball glass and garnish with an orange slice.

Traditional Margarita

Gold Margarita

Black Currant Margarita

Blackberry Margarita

Chambord Margarita

Cranberry Margarita

Citrus Margarita

Peach Margarita

Cowboy Margarita

Redheaded Stranger

Jumping Margarita

Icebreaker

Midori Margarita

Cherry Margarita

Pineapple Margarita

Piñata

Honeydew Margaritas

Passionfruit Margaritas

Frozen Strawberry Margaritas

Lavender Margaritas

Frozen Mango Margarita

Frozen Kiwi Margaritas

Frozen Watermelon Margaritas

Frozen Cherry Margaritas

4 margaritas

Traditional Margarita ▸

Serves 1

slice of lemon
salt
1½ oz tequila
1 oz Cointreau or triple sec
½ oz lime juice, freshly squeezed

Rub margarita glass rim with a lemon slice and frost with salt. Combine liquid ingredients with ice; shake well. Strain drink into glass. Garnish with a slice of lemon.

Variation: For a frozen margarita, blend 2 oz tequila, 1 oz of lime juice, 1 oz Cointreau or triple sec with 1 cup of crushed ice in a blender for 5-10 seconds until smooth. Serve immediately.

Gold Margarita

Serves 1

lime or lemon slice
½ oz Cointreau
salt
2 oz gold tequila
lime wedge, to garnish
1½ oz lime juice

Rub margarita glass rim with lime or lemon slice and frost with salt. Combine liquid ingredients with ice; shake well. Strain drink into glass. Garnish with lime wedge and serve.

Black Currant Margarita ▸

Serves 1

wedge of lime
salt
1½ oz tequila
1 oz crème de cassis liqueur
1½ oz lime juice
½ oz Cointreau or triple sec

Rub margarita glass rim with wedge of lime and frost with salt. Combine liquid ingredients with ice; shake well. Strain drink into glass. Garnish with a wedge of lime.

Blackberry Margarita

Serves 1

lemon or lime slice
1½ oz lime juice
salt
½ oz Cointreau
1½ oz tequila
lime wedge
1 oz blackberry liqueur

Rub margarita glass rim with lime or lemon slice and frost with salt. Combine liquid ingredients with ice; shake well. Strain drink into glass. Garnish with lime wedge and serve.

Chambord Margarita ▸

Serves 1

wedge of lime
salt
1½ oz tequila
1 oz lime or lemon juice
1 oz Chambord liqueur
½ oz Cointreau or triple sec

Rub margarita glass rim with lime wedge and frost with salt. Combine liquid ingredients with ice; shake well. Strain drink into glass. Garnish with a lime wedge.

Cranberry Margarita

Serves 1

lemon slice
1 oz triple sec
granulated sugar
2½ oz cranberry juice
1½ oz tequila
5 ice cubes
1 oz lemon juice
lemon slices, extra, to garnish

Rub margarita glass rim with lemon slice and frost with sugar. Combine liquid ingredients with ice; shake well. Pour drink into glass. Garnish with lemon slice and serve.

Citrus Margarita ▶

Serves 1

slice of lime
salt
2 oz tequila
1 oz lime juice, freshly squeezed
1 oz orange juice, freshly squeezed
1 oz Cointreau or triple sec
slice of orange

Rub margarita glass rim with lime slice and frost with salt. Combine liquid ingredients with ice; shake well. Strain drink into glass. Garnish with a slice of orange.

Peach Margarita

Serves 1

lime or lemon slice
1 oz peach liqueur
salt
$1/2$ oz Cointreau
$1^1/_2$ oz tequila
1 oz lime or lemon juice
lemon or lime slice, extra, to garnish

Rub margarita glass rim with lime or lemon slice and frost with salt. Combine liquid ingredients with ice; shake well. Strain drink into glass. Garnish with slice of lime or lemon and serve.

Cowboy Margarita ▸

Serves 4–6

1¹/₂ cups frozen limeade concentrate
1¹/₂ cups tequila
1¹/₂ cups beer

Place undiluted frozen limeade concentrate in a jug. Fill empty limeade can with tequila and pour into the jug. Fill empty limeade can with beer and pour into the jug. Serve over plenty of ice.

Redheaded Stranger

Serves 1

1 teaspoon medium-hot salsa
1 tablespoon pineapple purée
¹/₂ oz lime juice freshly squeezed
1 oz tequila
lime wedge

Drop the salsa into a 3 oz chilled cocktail glass. Next slowly pour in the pineapple purée. Gradually pour the lime juice over the back of a spoon into the cocktail, then repeat the process with the tequila. Suck on the lime wedge and sip the cocktail.

Jumping Margarita ▸

Serves 1

slice of lime
salt
1½ oz tequila
1 oz triple sec
1½ oz margarita mix
½ oz lime juice
3 oz lemonade
slice of lime, extra, for garnish

Rub margarita glass rim with lime slice and frost with salt. Mix the next 5 ingredients in shaker filled with ice; shake well. Strain cocktail into glass. Garnish with a slice of lime.

Icebreaker

Serves 1

2 oz tequila
2 oz grapefruit juice
1 teaspoon grenadine
½ oz Cointreau
crushed ice

Combine all ingredients in a blender and blend for a few seconds. Strain into a margarita glass.

Midori Margarita ▸

Serves 1

slice of lime or lemon slice
salt
2 oz tequila
1 oz lime or lemon juice
1 oz Midori
lemon or lime slice, extra, to garnish

Rub margarita glass rim with lime or lemon slice and frost with salt. Combine liquid ingredients with ice; shake well. Strain drink into glass. Garnish with a slice of lime or lemon.

Cherry Margarita

Serves 1

lime or lemon slice
salt
1 1/2 oz tequila
1 oz maraschino liqueur
1 1/2 oz lime juice, freshly squeezed
1/2 oz Cointreau
lime wedge, to garnish

Rub margarita glass rim with lime or lemon slice and frost with salt. Combine liquid ingredients with ice; shake well. Strain drink into glass. Garnish with lime wedge and serve.

Pineapple Margarita ▸

Serves 1

slice of lime or lemon
salt
2 oz tequila
2 oz pineapple juice
1 oz lime or lemon juice, freshly squeezed
1 oz Cointreau or triple sec
pineapple spear

Rub margarita glass rim with lime or lemon slice and frost with salt. Combine liquid ingredients with ice; shake well. Strain drink into glass. Garnish with pineapple spear and serve.

Piñata

Serves 1

1 oz tequila
$\frac{1}{2}$ oz banana liqueur
1 oz lime juice, freshly squeezed
crushed ice

Combine all ingredients with ice and shake well. Pour into a 3 oz cocktail glass.

Honeydew Margaritas ▸

Serves 2-4

slice of lime
salt
3 cups ripe honeydew melon, diced
1/4 cup gold tequila
2 oz triple sec
2 oz lime juice
14 large ice cubes
6 wedges of lime

Rub margarita glass rims with lime slice and frost with salt. Blend melon, tequila, triple sec, lime juice and ice cubes until slushy. Pour into prepared glasses, then garnish each with a lime wedge.

Passionfruit Margaritas

Serves 6

lime slices
12 oz tequila
salt
4 oz Grand Marnier
3 cups passionfruit juice
1 lime, freshly squeezed
raspberries, for garnish

Prepare glasses by rubbing margarita glass rims with lime slice and frost with salt. Combine liquid ingredients with ice; shake well. Store in the refrigerator until ready to use. Pour cocktail into glass over ice. Garnish with a few raspberries.

Frozen Strawberry Margaritas ▶

Serves 4

slices of lime or lemon
salt
³/₄ cup tequila
2 oz triple sec
¹/₄ cup frozen limeade concentrate
1 cup frozen strawberries
8 cups crushed ice

Rub margarita glass rim with lime or lemon slice and frost with salt. Combine ingredients in a blender and process until slushy. Pour drink into prepared glasses. Garnish with a slice of lime or lemon.

Lavender Margaritas

Serves 8–10

1 cup tequila
¹/₂ cup blue curacao
1 cup canned coconut milk
3 oz lime juice
1 lb frozen unsweetened raspberries
1 lb frozen unsweetened blueberries

4 cups ice cubes
1 tablespoon granulated sugar
1 teaspoon fresh lavender blossoms
lime wedge
lavender sprigs, rinsed (optional)

In a blender, combine tequila, curacao, coconut milk and lime juice. Cover and turn to high speed, then gradually add raspberries, blueberries and ice. Whirl until margarita mixture is smooth and slushy. Depending on the size of your blender bowl you may have to blend in batches. Put sugar and lavender blossoms in a saucer. Rub with your fingers or mash with a spoon to release some of the lavender flavor. Rub glass rims with lime wedge to moisten. Dip rims in lavender sugar, coating evenly. Pour margaritas into sugar-rimmed glasses. Garnish with lavender sprigs.

Frozen Mango Margarita ▶

Serves 1

wedge of lime
sugar
1½ oz silver tequila
1 oz triple sec
1½ oz lemon juice, freshly squeezed
2 oz Sweet-and-Sour Mix (see p. 4)
³/₄ cup mango, partially frozen
mango slice

Rub rim of glass with lime and frost with sugar. Mix all liquid ingredients with frozen mango and cracked ice in a blender and blend until slushy. Pour into prepared margarita glass and garnish with mango slice.

Frozen Kiwi Margaritas

Serves 2–4

lime slice
salt
½ cup silver tequila
½ cup triple sec
1 cup lemon juice, freshly squeezed
½ cup lime juice, freshly squeezed
½ cup sugar (superfine if available)
2 kiwis, peeled
crushed ice
lime wedges, to garnish

Rub margarita glass rims with lime slices and frost with salt. Put liquid ingredients, sugar and kiwifruit into a blender. On top of this mixture, pour crushed ice until blender is full. Blend until slushy. Pour into margarita glasses and garnish each with a lime wedge.

Frozen Watermelon Margaritas ▸

Serves 4

2 lbs seedless watermelon, cut into 1 in chunks
slice of lime
salt
$^3/_4$ cup tequila
$^1/_2$ cup triple sec
$2^1/_2$ oz fresh lime juice
4 wedges of lime

Place the melon chunks in a plastic bag, and freeze until solid. Rub 4 margarita glass rims with slice of lime and frost with salt. Transfer about three-quarters of the melon chunks, separating them, to a blender jar. Add the tequila, triple sec and lime juice and blend until fairly smooth. Add the remaining melon and ice and blend until smooth. Divide the cocktail mixture among the prepared glasses. Squeeze a lime wedge into each cocktail, drop the wedge into the glass, and serve immediately.

Frozen Cherry Margaritas

Serves 2–4

lime or lemon slice
1 oz lime juice
salt
1 oz maraschino liqueur

6 maraschino cherries
ice
$1^1/_2$ oz tequila
lime slices, extra, to garnish

Rub margarita glass rims with lime or lemon slice and frost with salt. In a blender, combine maraschino cherries, tequila, sugar, lime juice and maraschino liqueur. Blend until smooth. Add ice cubes a few at a time until the mixture becomes thick and slushy. Pour into prepared glasses. Garnish with lime or lemon slice and serve.

Liquid Measures

METRIC	IMPERIAL	CUP AND SPOON
millileters (mL)	**fluid ounce (fl oz)**	
5mL	$\frac{1}{6}$ fl oz	1 teaspoon
20mL	$\frac{2}{3}$ fl oz	1 tablespoon
30mL	1 fl oz	1 tbsp + 2 tsp
55mL	2 fl oz	
60mL	$2\frac{1}{4}$ fl oz	$\frac{1}{4}$ cup
85mL	3 fl oz	
115mL	4 fl oz	
125mL	$4\frac{1}{2}$ fl oz	$\frac{1}{2}$ cup
150mL	$5\frac{1}{4}$ fl oz	
190mL	$6\frac{2}{3}$ fl oz	$\frac{3}{4}$ cup
225mL	8 fl oz	
250mL	$8\frac{3}{4}$ fl oz	1 cup
300mL	$10\frac{1}{2}$ fl oz	
370mL	13 fl oz	
400mL	14 fl oz	
440mL	$15\frac{1}{2}$ fl oz	$1\frac{3}{4}$ cups
455mL	16 fl oz	
500mL	$17\frac{1}{2}$ fl oz	2 cups
570mL	20 fl oz	
1 liter	$35\frac{1}{3}$ fl oz	4 cups

Index

Page numbers in *italics* indicate illustrations.